All things bright and beautiful,
All creatures great and small,
All things wise and wonderful,
The Lord God made them all.

C. F. ALEXANDER

Copyright © MCMLXXXI by
The C.R. Gibson Company
Norwalk, Connecticut
All rights reserved
Printed in the United States of America
ISBN: 0-8378-2027-8

Because this page cannot accommodate all the copyright notices, the section in the back of the book designated "Acknowledgments" constitutes an extension of the copyright page.

All Things Bright and Beautiful

Words of Joy for Today

Selected by Stephanie C. Oda
Designed by Vicky-Jean Taloni

THE C.R. GIBSON COMPANY
NORWALK, CONNECTICUT

ALL THINGS BRIGHT AND BEAUTIFUL

*O Lord, how manifold
are thy works!*

PS. 104:24

Life has loveliness to sell,
*　　All beautiful and splendid things,*
Blue waves whitened on a cliff,
*　　Soaring fire that sways and sings,*
And children's faces looking up
Holding wonder like a cup.

SARA TEASDALE

Little drops of water,
*　　Little grains of sand,*
Make the mighty ocean
*　　And the pleasant land.*

Thus the little minutes,
*　　Humble though they be,*
Make the mighty ages
*　　Of eternity.*

JULIA FLETCHER CARNEY

Blossoms are scattered by the wind and the wind cares nothing, but the blossoms of the heart no wind can touch.

YOSHIDA KENKŌ

*Drink the brimming cup of life
to the full and to the end—
and thank God and nature
for its trials and challenges,
its punishments and rewards,
its gifts of beauty,
wisdom, labor and love.*

WILL DURANT

Do not stop thinking of life as an adventure.

ELEANOR ROOSEVELT

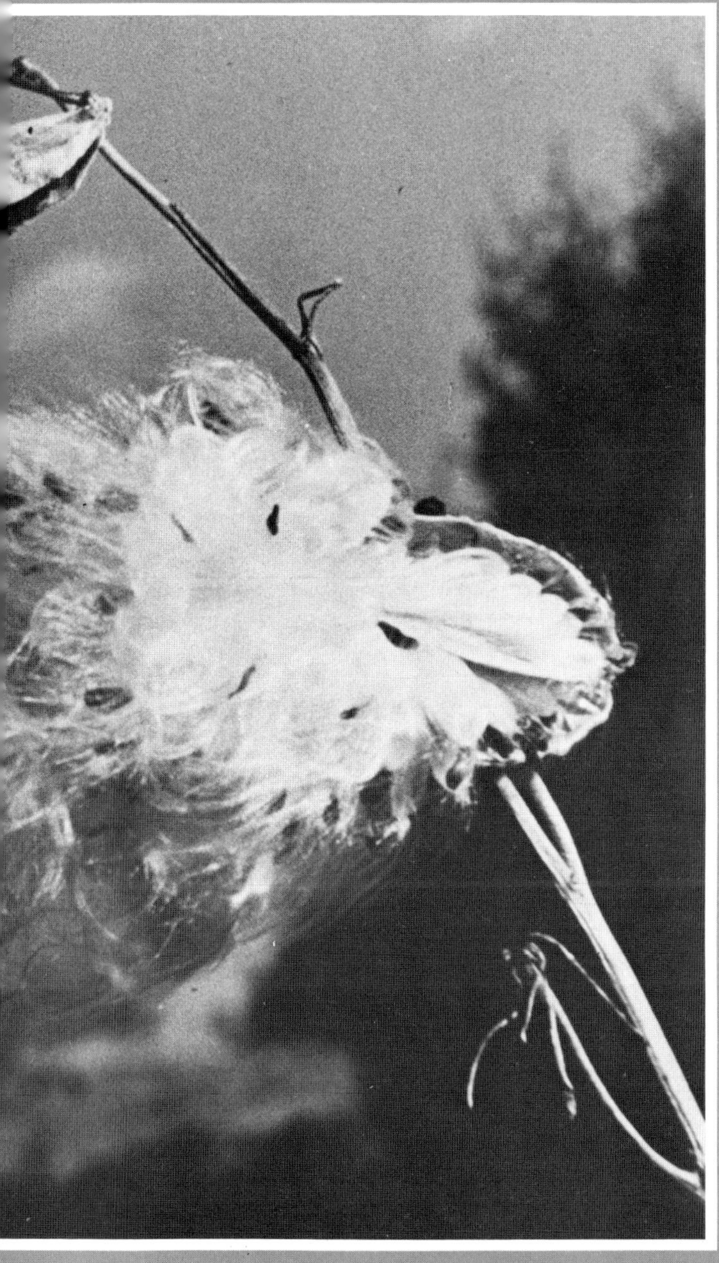

Begin at once to live, and count each day as a separate life.

A contributing factor to happiness is to be able to enjoy the gifts of nature. The poorest man living can enjoy these, for such blessings are free. Everybody can take pleasure in a glorious sunset. You would have to pay a great sum for a painting by a skilled artist. Only the wealthy can afford it, but almost any evening we can look at a brilliant western sky, and each one of us can say, "That's mine!"

DAVID O. MCKAY

The best way to know God is to love many things.

VINCENT VAN GOGH

ALL CREATURES GREAT AND SMALL

Four things on earth are small,
> but they are exceedingly wise:
the ants are a people not strong,
> yet they provide their food in the summer;
The badgers are a people not mighty,
> yet they make their homes in the rocks;
the locusts have no king,
> yet all of them march in rank;
the lizard you can take in your hands,
> yet it is in kings' palaces.

PROV. 30:24-28

I meant to do my work today
    But a brown bird sang in the apple tree,
And a butterfly flitted across the field,
    And all the leaves were calling me.

And the wind went sighing over the land,
    Tossing the grasses to and fro,
And a rainbow held out his shining hand—
    So what could I do but laugh and go?

RICHARD LE GALLIENNE

Dear Father, hear and bless
    Thy beasts and singing birds,
And guard with tenderness
    Small things that have no words.

ANONYMOUS

Consider the lilies of the field, how they grow; they neither toil nor spin; yet I tell you, even Solomon in all his glory was not arrayed like one of these.

MT. 6:28-30

*He prayeth well, who loveth well
Both man and bird and beast.*

*He prayeth best who loveth best
All things both great and small;
For the dear God who loveth us,
He made and loveth all.*

SAMUEL TAYLOR COLERIDGE

*Two white butterflies
Dance where, last winter, I saw
Two snowflakes vanish.*

JANE MERCHANT

We are not born as the partridge in the wood, or the ostrich of the desert, to be scattered everywhere; but we are to be grouped together, and brooded by love, and reared day by day in that first of churches, the family.

HENRY WARD BEECHER

*Laughter of children brings
The kitchen down with laughter.
While the old kettle sings
Laughter of children brings
To a boil all savory things.
Higher than beam or rafter,
Laughter of children brings
The kitchen down with laughter.*

BARBARA HOWES

*Pale, in the luminous wake of a star,
    You lie asleep with your fingers curled
In a puppy dog's fur, unaware that you are
    The light of a life, and the hope of the world.*

MARY WRIGHT LAMB

ALL THINGS WISE AND WONDERFUL

We know the truth, not only by the reason, but also by the heart.

BLAISE PASCAL

Walking down a country lane, a man heard his little granddaughter from the other side of a large bush. She was repeating the alphabet—A, B, C, D, E, but in an oddly reverent sort of way. He waited until she was through and then walked around to find her.
"What were you doing?" he asked.
"I was praying," she answered. "I couldn't think of the right words, so I just said the letters, and God will put them together into the words, because He knows what I was thinking."

ROBERT E. GOODRICH, JR.

*To see a world in a grain of sand
And a heaven in a wild flower,
Hold Infinity in the palm of your hand
And Eternity in an hour.*

WILLIAM BLAKE

Happiness sneaks in through a door you didn't know you left open.

JOHN BARRYMORE

The business of living calls for an occasional squeal of delight, and that comes only from being brought up short by something we may have dreamed about but certainly did not expect.

GEORGE KENT

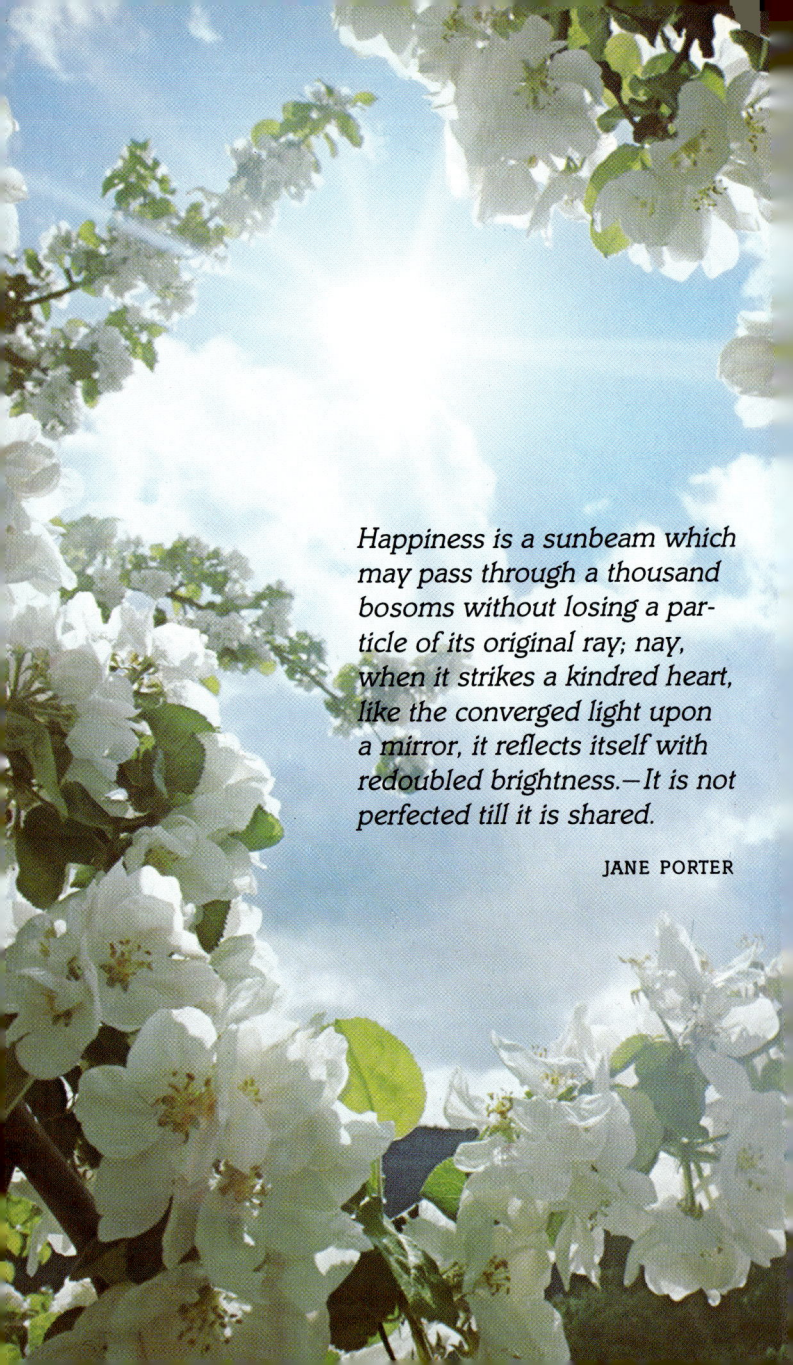

Happiness is a sunbeam which may pass through a thousand bosoms without losing a particle of its original ray; nay, when it strikes a kindred heart, like the converged light upon a mirror, it reflects itself with redoubled brightness.—It is not perfected till it is shared.

JANE PORTER

*Give us, Lord, a bit o' sun
A bit o' work and a bit o' fun;
Give us all in the struggle and sputter
Our daily bread and a bit o' butter;
Give us health, our keep to make,
An' a bit to spare for others' sake.
Give us sense, for we're some of us duffers,
An' a heart to feel for all that suffers;
Give us, too, a bit of song
And a tale, and a book to help us along.
An' give us our share of sorrow's lesson
That we may prove how grief's a blessin'.
Give us, Lord, a chance to be
Our goodly best for ourselves and others
Till all men learn to live as brothers.*

INSCRIBED ON THE WALL OF AN OLD
INN IN LANCASTER, ENGLAND.

THE LORD GOD MADE THEM ALL

For you shall go out in joy,
and be led forth in peace;
the mountains and the hills before you
shall break forth into singing,
and all the trees of the field shall
clap their hands.

IS. 55:12

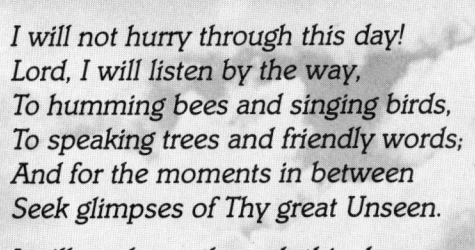

*I will not hurry through this day!
Lord, I will listen by the way,
To humming bees and singing birds,
To speaking trees and friendly words;
And for the moments in between
Seek glimpses of Thy great Unseen.*

*I will not hurry through this day;
I will take time to think and pray;
I will look up into the sky,
Where fleecy clouds and swallows fly;
And somewhere in the day, maybe
I will catch whispers, Lord, from Thee!*

RALPH SPAULDING CUSHMAN

The flowers of all the tomorrows are in the seeds of today.

JAPANESE PROVERB

*We thank you, Lord of Heaven,
For all the joys that greet us,
For all that you have given
To help us and delight us
In earth and sky and seas;
The sunlight on the meadows,
The rainbow's fleeting wonder,
The clouds with cooling shadows,
The stars that shine in splendor.
We thank you, Lord, for these.*

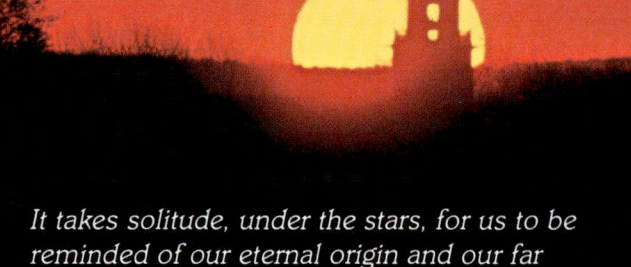

JAN STRUTHER

It takes solitude, under the stars, for us to be reminded of our eternal origin and our far destiny.

ARCHIBALD RUTLEDGE

I still find each day too short for all the thoughts I want to think . . . all the walks I want to take, all the books I want to read and all the friends I want to see. The longer I live, the more my mind dwells upon the beauty and wonder of the world.

JOHN BURROUGHS

ACKNOWLEDGMENTS

The editor and the publisher have made every effort to trace the ownership of all copyrighted material and to secure permission from copyright holders of such material. In the event of any question arising as to the use of any material the publisher and editor, while expressing regret for inadvertent error, will be pleased to make the necessary corrections in future printings. Thanks are due to the following authors, publishers, publications and agents for permission to use the material indicated.

ABINGDON PRESS, for an excerpt from *I Have A Stewardship* by Ralph Spaulding Cushman. Copyright renewal © 1967 by Maude E. Cushman; for an excerpt from *Because It's Here* by Jane Merchant. Copyright © 1970 by Jane Merchant.

DODD, MEAD & COMPANY, INC., for an excerpt from *The Lonely Dancer* by Richard Le Gallienne. Copyright © 1913 by Dodd, Mead & Company. Copyright © renewed 1941 by Richard Le Gallienne.

MACMILLAN PUBLISHING CO., INC., for an excerpt from *Collected Poems* by Sara Teasdale. Copyright © 1917 by Macmillan Publishing Co., Inc., renewed 1945 by Mamie T. Wheless.

NATIONAL COUNCIL OF THE CHURCHES OF CHRIST, for Ps. 104:24, Prov. 30:24-28, Mt. 6:28-30, Is. 55:12 from the *Revised Standard Version of the Bible.* Copyright © 1946, 1952, 1971, 1973.

OXFORD UNIVERSITY PRESS, for an excerpt by Jan Struther (1901-53) from *Enlarged Songs of Praise.*

READER'S DIGEST, for an excerpt from *The Shock of Happiness* by George Kent, Reader's Digest, March 1966.

FLEMING H. REVELL COMPANY, for an excerpt from *What's It All About?* by Robert E. Goodrich, Jr. Copyright © 1955 by Fleming H. Revell Company.

PHOTO CREDITS

Leslie Irvin—cover; Florida—pp.4,5; Bruce Ando—pp.6,7,18,19; Vermont—pp.8,9, acknowledgment page; Peter Haynes—p.10 insert; Jay Johnson—pp.10,11; James Patrick—pp.12,13,26,27, p.27 insert; Rosemarie Masucci—pp.14,15; Three Lions— pp.16,17,22,23; Phoebe Dunn—p.18 insert; Orville Andrews— pp.20,21; Gene Ruestmann—pp.24,25; end papers—Bruce Ando, Ed Cooper, Maria Demarest, Wanda Ensinger, Four By Five, Inc., Robert Grana, Jay Johnson, Maine, Jeff Munk, Wyoming.